The Podcast Host

~

Finally start your podcast
Become an indie podcaster
in 15-minute microsteps

Contents

Introduction

Why this book?

It's been ten years since the release of our original "How to start a podcast" book. In that time, there have been hundreds of similar books published, not to mention articles, videos, courses, and, of course, podcasts themselves. If you're looking for content on how to start your own show, then you'll never need to look far.

So why did we bother creating *yet another* body of content around the topic?

Well, there are a couple of reasons.

Firstly, as you can imagine, a lot has changed in ten years. There are new technologies, methods, and opportunities that simply weren't available back in 2013.

We've also learned a lot since then, both as a podcasting company, and as individuals who work and play in this medium, daily. I believe we have a very unique perspective on podcasting, drawing from a vast well of experience, and we'd be remiss not to share it with new and aspiring creators.

Secondly, we wanted to try something different with the format. It seems like the default approach when putting a book together is for it to read "like a novel". The reader starts at the start and gradually works through each page before finally arriving at the end. If you want to read this book in that way, then, brilliant. But, based on feedback we've had from our audience over the years, many folks were looking for something a little more distinct.

How to use this book

The terms "bite-sized", "pocket-sized", and "at a glance" would come up again and again in our conversations with early-stage podcasters. So this book is an attempt to provide that. The aim is that it's simple to find the stage you're working on, stuck in, or curious about, then get the no-fluff lowdown on it all.

Each section (or microstep) is a decision or task, and the idea is that, within about 15 minutes, you can either make a plan around it, implement it or disregard it altogether. You definitely don't need to do *everything* in this book, but we'll always give you the options as well as the facts.

There's no "fat" in this book - just the essential info you need to get clued up and on your way. And, wherever a deeper dive is required, we'll share free follow-up resources with you after covering the basics.

Finally start your podcast is a quick, accessible, and low-friction way of planning and growing a successful podcast. And, as the big aim is to save you as much time as possible, let's not waste any more of it getting to the meat.

Chapter one

Laying the foundations for success

So you're dying to hit record and get that first episode out there, but do you have your foundations in place? If you take a moment to figure out your ideal listener, the reason they'll be compelled to listen, and the format that suits them best, it'll put you in an optimal position to grow an audience.

In this chapter:
~ Why are you doing a podcast?
~ Who is your podcast for?
~ Why should they listen?
~ Niches & narrow podcast topics
~ Choosing a format for your podcast
~ The solo podcast format
~ The co-hosted podcast format
~ The interview podcast format
~ The roundtable podcast format
~ The documentary or fiction
  podcast format

Why are you doing a podcast?

We need to kick things off by asking the question, "Why?" Why do you want to make a podcast?

There are generally two camps here.

In the first, we have freelancers, thought leaders, or marketing department employees. In these instances, podcasting's a great way to build trust and authority. Plus, of course, give your customers or your audience a whole bunch of valuable and entertaining content.

In the second camp, we see more of a creative outlet, from hobbyists and connoisseurs to anyone who's passionate about a given topic. This could be anything from knitting or craft beer to horror movies or model railways.

Either way, it's important to figure out your "Why" right at the start.

It could be making more sales, growing a community, or getting famous! They're all valid. And they're essential to keep in mind so that you can stay motivated, even when life throws you those inevitable curveballs. Podcasting isn't always easy, but if your "Why" is worth it, you'll push on through.

Who is your podcast for?

The thing is, unless you know exactly *who* you're making your show for, and *why* you're doing it, you've got no chance of growing an audience.

Let's imagine a personal trainer who's making a health and fitness podcast to market their business. Their target audience might be people who are interested in healthy eating, weight loss, HIIT training, or bodybuilding.

Or, let's imagine a hobbyist who loves zombies and post-apocalyptic fiction. Their target audience would simply be folks with the same really specific passion. They might be fans of TV shows like *The Walking Dead*, and video games like *Resident Evil.*

It's a good idea to sketch out what's known as your "avatar". An avatar is a made-up person that represents your ideal listeners in the real world. Your avatar should have a name, age, job, background, likes, and dislikes. You make this as real as you can, so it's someone you can know, deeply. The benefit then is that, with each episode you plan out, you can ask yourself the question, "Would Jane (my avatar) like this?"

Asking that question is the key to making really compelling content, every time.

For a detailed look at how to create your avatar, and a bunch of examples, go to thepodcasthost.com/avatar

Why should they listen?

This, my friend, is all about supplying value in your very own unique way. But what does that *actually* mean?

Well, let's take the example of our personal trainer I mentioned last time. If they're serving up content that helps their listeners to, let's say, complete a couch to 5k, then they're providing value. If they can help a listener lose a few stones, or run a faster race, then that's a LOT of value!

Or what about our zombie podcaster? They might do an in-depth interview with a top author in the space. They'll dig in to unearth some anecdotes and insights that you've never heard anywhere else before from that writer. In that, they're providing some really unique value.

If you do something similar on your show, not only have you given your audience a reason to listen, but you've also given them a reason to come back for more, every week.

This is absolutely vital for you to think about in the planning stages. So, can you write down 10-15 potential episodes that you think your target audience would love to listen to? If you're teaching, it's often about considering the most common problems you can help them solve. And if it's entertainment, it's finding new content or entertainment that scratches that person's personal itch.

And, for a more detailed look at giving them a reason to listen, go to thepodcasthost.com/unique

Niches & narrow podcast topics

There's a bit of a misconception in podcasting that the broader and more open your topic, the bigger your audience will be.

I know, it makes sense because covering lots of ground means there are loads more people who *might* be interested in your show.

The reality, though, is that listeners love podcasts that feel like they were made *just for them*.
So instead of our personal trainer doing a podcast about general health, diet, or exercise, it might be "the fitness podcast for single parents", or "the keto diet podcast for vegetarians".

In other areas, niche podcasts could be "The travel podcast, for D&D players", or "The business startup podcast, for military veterans".

You might have a fear that this will limit your audience, but, actually, the opposite is true. When your target listeners find your show and see how closely it scratches their itch, they'll think, "This is perfect!", hit 'Follow', and go on to become fanatical fans. On the other hand, if keep it general, everyone just sees it, goes 'meh' and moves on.

When you try to target everyone, you really target no one in particular.

So what would you rather have - a tight, defined group of fanatical listeners, or a big group who just *might* be interested in listening?

For a really detailed look at defining your niche topic, go to thepodcasthost.com/topic

Choosing a format for your podcast

The format you choose is really personal and depends on who's involved. If it's just you, you're not doing a co-hosted show any time soon, for example.

None of this is set in stone, either. So whilst it's good to have an 'average' format, so your listeners know what to expect, you don't have to stick to it every single time.

You might do your first few episodes using a certain format – for example, solo - then decide it isn't for you. In this case, you could pivot and start doing interviews. Or, you could bring on a regular co-host.

The first format you try might feel perfectly natural to you, in which case, great. Or you might opt for a 'mixed bag' approach where you never stick to any one set format. The beauty of it is that it's *your* podcast, and you get to make the rules.

Let's kick on now and dig into the pros and cons of each podcast format.

The solo podcast format

The big benefit of a solo show is that you don't need to rely on anyone else to record your episodes. On top of that, it's YOU who's building a reputation as the authority on your subject.

The podcast is also exclusively yours, so you can make all the calls on sponsorship and monetisation. And you don't need to split the profits with anyone

There are potential downsides, too, though. A solo podcast is perhaps the most intimidating style of show for a beginner. One of the biggest challenges of flying solo is getting over the feeling that you're 'talking to yourself' and realising that you're actually talking to your listener.

"A solo podcast is perhaps the most intimidating style of show for a beginner."

The co-hosted podcast format

This is when you present your show alongside another regular host - whether it's a friend or a colleague.

This is an excellent format for anyone, but particularly early podcasters. It reduces that 'mic fright' you get when recording solo, or the possibility of being a bit monotone. Instead, find the right co-host, and you can have a totally natural conversation. Someone to bounce off, debate with, or even take the mickey out of.

The best co-hosted podcasts have great chemistry between the presenters. You end up being a fly on the way to a great, funny, informative conversation. That creates a first-class listening experience.

As always, though, there are challenges. Suddenly you have to coordinate with someone else's calendar when you arrange to record, for example.

Then, there's the question of ownership: whose podcast is it? Do you split any future income 50/50? And what happens if your co-host loses interest or just can't do it in the future?

So if you do opt for this style of show, definitely have that conversation with your co-host up front, before hitting record on your first episode.

The interview podcast format

This is where you 'borrow' the expertise or entertainment value of others. With this style of podcast format, a huge benefit is getting to talk to your heroes.

Here, you'll have the opportunity to have a chat with people in your space that you've always looked up to. On top of that, your guests will have their own audiences who may listen to the interview and end up following your show. If done right, you can really grow an audience this way.

On the flip side, interviewing is a skill that you'll need to hone through practice, so don't approach the A-listers in your field straight away.

There are other challenges, too. You'll need to constantly find and approach potential guests, schedule interviews, and rely on others to show up – either in-person or digitally. And, you'll also need to rely on the technology to work properly throughout each call.

The roundtable podcast format

A "roundtable" refers to the idea of getting a larger number of participants together to discuss a set topic. Usually, there would be at least one regular host, if not two or three. Then the rest of the 'table' is made up of guests who are experts in the topic at hand.

Your job as host is to direct the roundtable, asking questions and steering the topic, so that everyone gets a turn and contributes to a great conversation.

The roundtable format can be a good way to build authority in your niche. This allows you to invite prominent guests to the show who'll share their wisdom and experience.

That said, organising multiple guests and finding suitable recording times can be a big challenge. Each person you add to the mix adds another layer of complexity. Only the most organised people can pull this off in the long run.

The documentary or fiction podcast format

Documentary podcasts are often called "BBC-style" or "NPR-style". These shows mix in multiple voices, musical elements, and actuality to add an extra layer of production and storytelling. The end product can sound great, but the time and work needed to put them together will increase drastically.

Another high-production format is the fiction podcast. These come in many forms, from "audiobook style" to fully soundscaped audio dramas, where every footstep is accounted for. Again, the result can be fantastic, but running a fiction podcast is a big time investment, especially if you want to publish episodes on a regular basis.

Of course, the reward for such a heavy workload is that these shows can *really* stand out, which helps them to grow fanatical audiences.

They also make great showcases for many skill sets, from writing and storytelling to recording and production. Some fiction podcasts have even been adapted into TV shows!

Chapter two

Names, descriptions & art

Names are always hard, so let's dig into how to choose a great one. Then, we'll nail down your format, from length, to frequency and beyond.

In this chapter:
~ How to name your podcast
~ Choosing a descriptive podcast name
~ Choosing a clever, quirky, or mysterious podcast name
~ Using your own name in your podcast name
~ How long should my podcast episodes be?
~ How often should I release podcast episodes?
~ Why podcast in seasons?
~ How should I name my podcast episodes?
~ What should go in my podcast description?
~ How to find good podcast cover art

How to name your podcast

There are three main camps when it comes to naming your show - you might simply base it on your name, or you might opt for something clever or descriptive. We're going to look at each option, in more depth, over the next few sections.

Start by creating a shortlist of potential podcast names. Then, search a directory or app like Apple Podcasts to see if any of them are taken.

If your perfect show name is being used by a podcast that stopped publishing episodes ten years ago, then this can be frustrating.

Of course, there are plenty of shows out there with the same name as one another - however, it's better not to cause confusion to your audience by joining their ranks.

So try to come up with something new and unique here. That will ultimately give your podcast the best chance of being discovered and growing to its maximum potential.

Choosing a descriptive podcast name

Famous examples of descriptive names are The Property Podcast and Football Weekly. This type of name can be described as "doing exactly what it says on the tin".

You might think of this as the "boring" option, but as long as your content isn't boring, nobody's going to care.

Descriptive podcast names are immediately identifiable to their target audience. And they're easier to find because they perform better in searches.

However, if you have a creative or clever name picked out for your show and are desperate to use it, you can always find a way to merge it with a descriptive title, too. Is there a pun or reference in your niche that you could work into your show's name somehow? An example of this might be 'Field of Dreams: The Sleep Therapist's Podcast'.

Choosing a clever, quirky, or mysterious podcast name

Famous examples here include The Moth, and 99% Invisible. Creative or "clever" names are often built around puns, plays on words or in-jokes from the show's topic or niche.

Many of these names make sense when you look deeply enough into them. But others are just plain abstract and offer no hint of the show's actual content.

If you already have an audience, a reputation as a good content creator, or a big marketing budget, then this won't necessarily hold you back. If enough people check out your show and enjoy it, then you'll do fine.

But if you're starting completely from scratch, then you need to ask yourself what your target audience is searching for online – and if your podcast name is going to show up in these searches.

Does this sound more like your own situation? If so, then you might want to opt for the descriptive naming route instead!

Using your own name in your podcast name

If you've heard of Tim Ferriss or Joe Rogan, you'll know what we're talking about here. Podcasts named after their hosts generally have one thing in common – the host already had an audience *before* they started the podcast.

These names offer no hints about the show's content. If you've never heard of Tim Ferris, his show could be about literally anything.

As it happens, the podcast is about "interviewing world-class performers" in all fields, linking the similarities and routines that connect them.

If nobody knew Tim Ferris, he'd probably have put more description into his title. Something like "How to be World Class" would certainly catch the eye of his target audience.

So if you already have a strong personal brand, then this can work well for you. If you're a bit more early-stage, though, then opt for a more descriptive podcast name instead.

How long should my podcast episodes be?

Here's the bottom line - podcast length depends solely on content. Don't cut down good content - or pad out succinct work!

How long does your episode need to be to get the message out? Then that's the ideal length for you.

If you asked most podcast listeners, a "short" episode would probably be anything under 15 minutes. And a "long" episode would probably be anything over an hour.

Anything from 20 to 45 minutes seems to be the "typical" episode length, but again, let your content dictate.

Just try to aim for some ballpark consistency from episode to episode. Doing 5mins one week, and then 2 hours the next, is going to be a bit jarring for your audience. Podcast listeners like to know what to expect!

For a deeper dive into this topic, head on over to thepodcasthost.com/length

How often should I release podcast episodes?

Just like the "ideal length" question, there's no one-size-fits-all answer here. The best podcast release schedule is really the most regular one that *you* can stick to on a consistent basis.

So, if you can only manage once a month, that's fine. If you can manage every two weeks, even better. If you can manage weekly, then that's about ideal.

You can still have a big impact with a fortnightly, or monthly show, but people plan their lives around what day of the week it is. It's the routine at the forefront of our lives, so tapping into a weekly release schedule can build a strong habit in your listeners.

And what about daily podcasts? These shows tend to have shorter episodes and are often batch produced. That means planning, recording, and scheduling a week or two's worth in just one day. So they can actually be *more* sustainable in certain cases. But, as always, it depends entirely on what works best for you and for your listeners. Does your audience really want what you're offering every day? Or would they prefer something deeper, once a week?

Ultimately, remember that it's down to quality. Sticking to a deadline which reduces the quality of your episodes is pointless. You'll have a bigger impact if you put out one excellent episode a month instead of a totally average episode every week, or even - every day.

"Ultimately, remember that it's down to quality."

Why podcast in seasons?

Now we know more about the tricky balance of finding your ideal release frequency. So, what if the podcast you'd like to create is a really in-depth, highly-produced show, that goes out every single week? But, you know that, in the long run, that weekly schedule is a bit unsustainable?

The ideal answer could be to take a leaf out of your favourite TV show's book and podcast in seasons.

Here, a "season" represents a block of episodes. The "How many" is up to you. For some, it'll be six, for others, it'll be upwards of 20. This means that you can really throw yourself into creating some great content and then take a well-deserved rest before going on to tackle the next season.

The beauty of this approach is that seasons can be "themed", which makes your show accessible and appealing to new listeners. Our fitness podcaster, for example, might do an entire season on upper body strength, whilst our zombie podcaster could do one on post-apocalyptic video games.

Podcasters who take this "themed season" approach also benefit from repurposing and monetising their content. We've seen many ebooks and courses created from them because a lot of the work in the planning, structure, and organisation has already been done.

One common critique of seasons is that listeners will "forget about you" during your breaks. This doesn't need to be the case. So long as you make it clear to them how the show works and how long the break is, then they'll know what to expect. You're also asking them to follow you on their listening app of choice, too. So they never need to "remember" you've come back - your next episode will be delivered to them automatically, without any effort on their part. Sell that benefit to them, and all will be well!

For a more detailed look at podcasting in seasons, go to thepodcasthost.com/seasons

How should I name my podcast episodes?

We spent a bit of time earlier talking about what to call your podcast as a whole. But how you title your episodes can be just as - or maybe even more - important!

The biggest mistake when naming your episodes is to pop in meaningless details. Think "Episode 13 - A Conversation With…" etc. Here, you've already lost them before they find out the topic.

Instead, you need to front-load the title with value, really give them a reason to listen. What's the meat of the episode? What problem are you solving? What solution are you offering? This is a big clue as to what your episode title should be. That's what draws people in.

We find a lot of good *and* bad examples of episode titles with interview shows. If you have a guest on, don't just call the episode "A Chat with Jane Smith". If your listener has never heard of Jane, why would they care?

But as it happens, Jane could be an expert on something they're really struggling with, so this would be the perfect episode for them. It's your duty as a host to signpost the value to them as much as possible.

The added benefit of descriptive episode titles is that they'll show up in search in most listening apps. So if someone types in a "how to" question on your own topic, and you have an episode on it, then there's a much better chance of them finding your show. Everyone wins!

For a more detailed look at naming your podcast episode, go to thepodcasthost.com/episodetitles

What should go in my podcast description?

Did you know that this is THE most important thing potential new listeners will judge your show on? This is in that crucial period where they've found it but haven't hit play yet.

By the way, that's not my opinion - it comes right from the horse's mouth via our Podcast Discovery Survey, which you can find at thepodcasthost.com/discovery

So, a quick bit of clarity on what's meant by "podcast description" - this is the summary of your podcast in its entirety. So don't confuse it with the shownotes that accompany each episode.

Podcast descriptions are often written as an afterthought, but they're worth spending a good bit of time on. In them, you should talk about *who* the show is for and what they can expect from it. We've covered this already in our "who" and "why" sections, so you've done the groundwork here - now, you just need to make it clear to your would-be listeners.

You'll also want to let them know what to expect regarding format and schedule. Do new episodes drop each Friday? Or do new seasons run every second month?

Of course, you probably want to mention a bit about yourself, too. For example, who you are, what your angle is and why you're doing this show. Credibility is good, but the big key here is to make it all about *them* - the listeners. Just imagine someone reading it and thinking to themselves, "What's in this for *me*?".

For a more detailed look at writing the perfect summary for your show, go to thepodcasthost. com/description

How to find good podcast cover art

Just like your episode titles, first impressions are everything. Having attractive cover art that stands out is vital when your show lines up against thousands of others in apps like Apple Podcasts and Spotify.

Your artwork should be at least 1400 x 1400 pixels, in JPG form, and it needs to be under 500kb in size. Apple actually recommends 3000 x 3000-pixel files, but we've found because they're much weightier, those big files can cause issues with your RSS feeds further down the line. So I'd usually opt for the smaller formats to help avoid running into the same problem.

Your artwork will normally be viewed as a thumbnail - pretty small on-screen, often on a phone - so don't cram any small text onto it. In fact, the *only* text on there would ideally be your podcast name. I often think that simpler is better with artwork. A textbook example would be your podcast title, covering practically the whole space, with your brand colours and a background image, or a really small illustration alongside.

You can create decent cover art for free on Canva. They even have podcast logo templates on there. Or, you might want to hire a freelancer on a platform like Fiverr if you'd like someone to do it for you. The benefit of working with a designer is that they can help you to encapsulate your branding. Cover art is a bit like choosing a podcast name in many ways. You're trying to find that balance between descriptiveness, cleverness, and quirkiness, all in one static image - and it all still needs to work well when viewed as a thumbnail on a phone screen.

For a more detailed look at designing your perfect podcast logo, go to thepodcasthost.com/art

Chapter three

Equipment & sound quality

There's no need to turn yourself into an audio engineer to make a great podcast. Here, we'll guide you through the choppy waters of gear and recording environments, so that you can capture crystal-clear audio in the simplest way possible.

In this chapter:
~ What's the deal with podcast equipment?
~ Podcast equipment for solo shows
~ Podcast equipment for online interviews or co-hosts
~ Podcast equipment for multiple local participants
~ What is a condenser microphone?
~ What is a dynamic microphone?
~ What are polar patterns?
~ Why does your recording environment matter?
~ How to eliminate reverb in any room
~ Background noise: sound treatment vs sound proofing
~ Should you record outdoors?

What's the deal with podcast equipment?

When we hear the term "podcast equipment", it's easy to imagine a pro-level studio filled with lots of intimidating and very expensive kit. But for most podcasters, this looks nothing like their own recording setup.

You can break podcast equipment into categories based on how you record and capture your voice, from mic to mixer to recorder to computer.

The recording process can be as simple or as complicated as you like. You can record right into your computer, ridding yourself of the need for a mixer or a recorder. Or you can go the full studio route and use it all.

If you use very little kit, the process will be simple, but you'll also have less flexibility and control. This isn't an issue for most aspiring podcasters, though, as they've no intention of becoming an audio engineer – they just want to get their message out there.

There is no "one-size-fits-all" podcast equipment recommendation. As we covered earlier, there are a few different podcast format options, and the format you choose will have a bearing on what gear you need.

As will, of course, your budget. So over the next few sections, we'll take a look at some common use cases and give you recommendations for each of them. On top of that, we'll give you a few easy-to-understand explanations of gear-related terms you'll likely come across, too.

For a more detailed look at choosing the right kit for you and your podcast, go to thepodcasthost.com/equipment

Podcast equipment for solo shows

If you're podcasting on your own, then this makes choosing equipment easy. You're just going to need a USB mic and some headphones. I say "headphones", but even your trusty earbuds will do the trick here.

You'll use these to "monitor" yourself as you record. That way, you can hear exactly *what* you record, as it's recorded, and pick up on any sound issues there and then.

On the USB mic front, it seems like there are hundreds of quality and good value options on the market these days. This can make choosing one tricky. With that in mind, we're just going to recommend the one we think is ideal for 98% of aspiring and early-stage podcasters - the Samson Q2U.

The Q2U can usually be bought brand new on Amazon for less than $70. You can also buy it in a special podcasting bundle with headphones and a boom arm for around $95 - which is an excellent deal.

Aside from being a great-sounding budget mic, the Q2U works in both USB AND XLR form, so if you want to upgrade to a mixer or digital recorder further down the line, you won't need to spend more money on a new mic.

The Samson Q2U's availability varies depending on where you are in the world, but an almost identical mic is the ATR2100, so keep that in mind if you have trouble getting your hands on a Q2U.

For a more detailed look at the Samson Q2U as the ideal solo podcaster mic, go to thepodcasthost.com/solo

Podcast equipment for online interviews or co-hosts

Typically, the set-up here is exactly the same as if you were podcasting on your own, and the Samson Q2U works just as well for remote recordings as it does on the solo front.

You'd then use online recording software or additional equipment to link up with your guests or co-hosts. We'll cover software in-depth in a future section, so let's focus on equipment for now.

The Zoom PodTrak P4 is a great little podcast recorder that lets you plug in multiple mics and record calls (both phone AND online). You can even play music and sound effects "as live" in your recordings, too.

For most people, though, using call recording software is the best option because of its pure simplicity.

But if you *do* fancy getting yourself a Zoom PodTrak P4, they're usually available for less than $200 on Amazon.

This will give you the option to do remote recordings AND in-person recordings, as we'll cover next.

Podcast equipment for multiple local participants

If getting people in the same room together is the key to your podcast, then there are a few different options out there.

I've already mentioned the Samson Q2U mic and the Zoom PodTrak P4 podcast recorder. As it happens, these can be great options for local in-person sessions, too. Get yourself a PodTrak P4 and then a Q2U for each person you'll be recording, and you'll have a brilliant setup for only a few hundred dollars.

With the PodTrak P4, you don't need a computer, as it records independently. If you'd prefer to record on a computer, you could get a USB audio interface and plug your mics into that. My favourite USB audio interface is the Focusrite Scarlett 2i2, but be mindful that this only runs two mics simultaneously.

A few more high-end options, if you have a bit of budget behind you, are the Zoom H6 digital recorder and the Rodecaster Pro podcast recorder. These are premium options, and if you pair them with mics like the Rode Procaster or Shure SM7B, then you'll have a better setup than 99% of other podcasters out there.

Of course, there's no need to spend a fortune on your podcasting kit, so for most folks, a handful of Samson Q2Us running into a Zoom PodTrak P4 will be more than good enough.

For a more detailed look at the Zoom PodTrak P4 as a podcast recorder option, go to thepodcasthost.com/podtrakp4

What is a condenser microphone?

"Condenser" and "Dynamic" are two of the most common types of mic. The terms refer to how they're built and how they function.

We can get really technical with stuff like this, but I'd rather keep it simple. That means I'll make some generalisations that aren't *always* the rule – now and then, you'll find exceptions.

But here's a good starting point for differentiating between the two.

A Condenser mic can be looked at as primarily something you'd use to record vocals in a professional studio environment.

Condenser microphones can often be more sensitive and easier to break.

Their sensitivity means they tend to pick up more sounds from around your recording environment. This can be a pro or a con, depending on what you're trying to do. Most are designed for more permanent setups on mic stands or boom arms, as opposed to being carried around and shoved in and out of boxes or bags.

A Condenser mic is powered either by having its own battery, or by using a function called *Phantom Power* on your mixer, preamp, or recorder.

This is why Condenser mics can usually record at a much lower gain than dynamics. Gain is essentially your input recording volume. The outcome is that a lower gain means less hiss in your recording.

Condenser mics often have multiple polar pattern options, making them versatile for different recording needs and setups.

What is a dynamic microphone?

Dynamic microphones tend to be tougher and more durable than their Condenser counterparts. A Dynamic mic can be seen as something you'd use in "live" environments and rougher "on-the-go" settings.

If you record live, on-location, or just like having a mic on you at all times for ad-hoc recordings, then a Dynamic mic is a great option.

Most Dynamic mics only have a cardioid polar pattern, however, which means they're generally designed for single-person use. If you're using Dynamics for interviews, then you'd either need to get two, or hold one in your hand and constantly point it back and forward.

Dynamic mics are powered by whatever they're plugged into, meaning the recording signal isn't as strong as it would be with a Condenser.

This means you either need to turn the gain up more or bring the recording level up in the post-production/editing process. Either way, that will raise the level of hiss in your audio. But this is far from a deal breaker, and often, the pros outweigh the cons with Dynamic mics in podcasting.

Our most recommended mic, the Samson Q2U, is a Dynamic model, which means it's durable, flexible, and doesn't require a perfect environment to sound good either. That's what makes it such a good option for beginners on a limited budget!

For a deeper dive on this topic, head on over to thepodcasthost. com/dynamicvcondenser

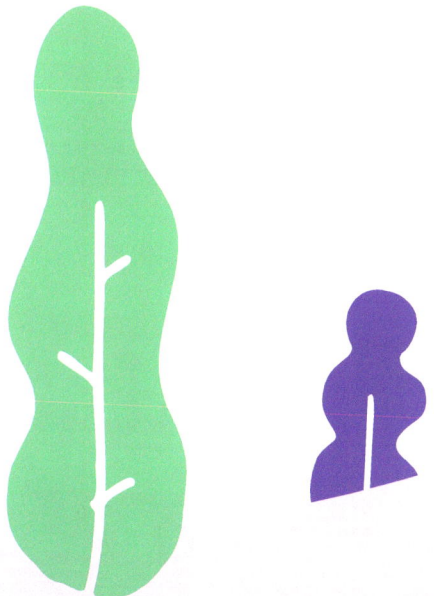

What are polar patterns?

These are also sometimes called "pickup patterns", and they're essentially the settings that determine the area a mic will focus on when recording sound.

To think about this visually, imagine your mic as a torch or laser. The area it shines a light on is the area it's "hearing" your voice.

Most microphones you'll come across - including the Samson Q2U - have a 'Cardioid' polar pattern which means they're designed to record one person at once.

Other polar patterns include:

- Omnidirectional - for recording multiple people.
- Bi-directional, or, Stereo - for recording two people.
- And Shotgun - for a laser-focused pickup of an audio source that blocks out everything else around it. Think of a news reporter, chatting away in a busy street, but you can still hear them clear as day.

Polar patterns are represented by easy-to-understand diagrams. For example, Cardioid is heart-shaped, whilst Omnidirectional is a circle. These are like birds-eye views of where the pattern is picking up sound.

To get a look at these diagrams and to learn more about polar patterns in general, head on over to thepodcasthost.com/patterns

Why does your recording environment matter?

It's easy to think that your equipment determines your audio quality - and, to an extent, that's true. But the room or place you record in has a much bigger impact on how your content will sound.

There are two main factors in your environment affecting your audio. Firstly, there's the "sound" of the room itself. Echo or reverb can be a real problem for podcasters, and we'll take a look at it in more depth in the next section (including a tip to kill it in *any* room for less than $15).

The other factor is noise. Now, I'm not saying for a minute that you should have complete and utter silence when you record - very few people have that luxury - and, in the right context, some gentle background noise can add ambience and atmosphere.

The key is, though, that background noise should never be distracting or compete with your actual voice. Your listeners should always be able to hear and focus on the content and message they've turned up for.

If they can't do that, after all, then the whole thing's going to fall apart.

For a more detailed look at podcast recording environments, go to thepodcasthost.com/homestudio

How to eliminate reverb in any room

Excess reverb can make even the best podcast sound amateur. This unwanted echo effect happens in smaller, boxy rooms with many hard surfaces. Here, the sound waves of your voice will bounce around the room like a ball.

Typically poor-sounding environments include caves, the bottoms of wells, and the average person's bathroom. It's unlikely you plan to record in any of these, but the room you've set aside for your recordings might actually sound like it's one of them. So, what can we do about it?

Well, you could simply record somewhere else. Typically, bedrooms are softer-sounding environments. Some podcasters swear by recording in their closets, for example.

Alternatively, you can create temporary recording havens by using duvets, towels, or dedicated acoustic blankets. The beauty of these is that they can be tidied away afterwards, if space is at a premium in your home.

If you have the luxury of a more permanent setup, you can buy acoustic foam tiles at a reasonable price and stick them to the walls, and even, the roof of your room. The thing is, though, you don't actually need to sound treat entire rooms - you only need to deal with the small area where you and your mic are set up.

My favourite trick here is to buy a cat bed. You'll get one of these in the pet shop for less than $15, and they make excellent little "studios" to place your mic in. Then, you just talk into it, and your audio will be free from reverb - even if you *are* recording down a well.

Background noise: Sound treatment vs sound proofing

Let's clear up a bit of confusion amongst podcasters - the difference between sound *treatment* and sound *proofing*.

In the last section, we talked about reverb, and that's very much in the sound *treatment* camp. But many folks mistakenly believe that, once they've stuck up some acoustic tiles, they have sound *proofed* their room.

If Dave Grohl were to move into the flat next door and start playing his drums, you'd quickly find out that your room hasn't been sound proofed at all, though.

Eliminating unwanted background noise can be harder than *treating* the sound of a room, for obvious reasons. There are some low-hanging fruits, though. Getting rid of that annoying clock, closing a window, or giving Dave next door a crisp 20 to nip down the pub for the next hour.

The good news is that most unwanted background noise will be too minimal to be picked up by your mic and cause any distractions on your audio. A dynamic, cardioid microphone like the Samson Q2U, for example, does a great job of rejecting unwanted sounds around you.

So do your best to minimise background noise, but don't obsess over it. Conditions will rarely be perfect, after all. And you can't let them get in the way of your progress as a podcaster.

For a more detailed look at dealing with background noise in podcasting, go to thepodcasthost.com/noise

Should you record outdoors?

In the previous few sections, we've talked about the importance of good recording environments. Well, one of the best is actually right outside your window. I'm talking, of course, about the great outdoors.

If you're plagued by reverb, loud distracting background noise, or a simple lack of space, then I'd encourage you to try recording your next episode whilst out on a walk, or sitting on your favourite park bench.

Sure, there can be plenty "noise" outside. But this often works in an ambient sense, rather than a distracting or annoying one.

Recording outdoors can also help with your presentation style. If you're out a walk, the blood is flowing, and you tend to feel more energetic, too. This is especially good if you suffer a bit from "mic fright" or lack of confidence.

Equipment-wise, your smartphone can work well with the right recording app. Or, you might want to get yourself a digital recorder and lavalier mic.

We take a deeper dive into some gear recommendations, additional tips, and case studies at thepodcasthost.com/outdoors

Chapter four

Your podcast software stack

Software can be simple if you choose the right route. From recording and editing to transcriptions, and even, AI, let's take a look at some of the best options on the market.

In this chapter:
~ Podcast software
~ Remote call recording options
~ What are daws? digital audio workstations
~ 'Podcast Maker' tools
~ Why use transcription?
~ Where to get your podcast transcribed
~ AI software

Podcast software

The term "Podcast software" is commonly used to describe the programme or app you use to record, edit, or publish your episodes. Some platforms only focus on one of these aspects, whilst others will do all three.

It's common for editing software to double up as recording software. Prime examples of these are Audacity, Adobe Audition, and our own Alitu. Many online call recorders don't have editing functions, though (or, if they do, they tend to be very basic).

Podcast publishing or hosting software might also offer basic recording and editing features. We'll take a deeper dive into some options here in a future section.

Transcription is also important from an accessibility and legal point of view. There are plenty of software options on that front, too, as we'll soon find out.

You might even think of your project management or scheduling tools as podcast software. These are tools like Trello, Asana, Notion, Calendly, and Book Like a Boss.

So there's no shortage of "podcast software" types to learn about here. Let's crack on.

Remote call recording options

Many podcasters run interview or co-hosted shows, and with call recording software, location is no barrier to who you can chat with.

Online call recorders do exactly what they say on the tin. Two of the most popular options out there are Squadcast and Riverside. These are what's known as "double ender" tools which record each participant locally, on their own computer. This makes them safer from wonky wifi connections and crashes, and the sound quality is generally better, too. They also both record video as well as audio.

On top of that, our own Alitu has a call recorder feature - one that we're constantly working on and improving. The big benefit of using Alitu is that it handles all of the syncing, processing, cleaning up, and volume levelling automatically. Its editing tools are also powerful, but at the same time, stupidly simple to use.

Of course, everyone on the planet has spent the past few years using Zoom, and you can use that to record remote calls too. You just need the right software and know-how to edit and mix them into decent-sounding episodes afterwards.

For a deeper look at remote recording software options, go to thepodcasthost.com/ onlinerecording

What are DAWs Digital audio workstations

A DAW is a term used to describe the software you use to record, edit, and produce audio. Most of them are designed and built with music production in mind, but can work brilliantly to create spoken-word content if you know what you're doing.

A famous free DAW is Audacity. Audacity is popular because of its price, or lack of one. It has everything you need to record and produce a podcast, but it suffers from looking a bit clunky and dated.

Adobe Audition, Reaper, and Hindenburg are three other popular options among podcasters. These are all paid DAWs, but they're a definite improvement on Audacity. The downside of DAWs tends to be their steep learning curve. Because they're so powerful and flexible, they can take a lot of time and effort to learn, even at a basic level. Most DAWs don't work as remote call recorders either, unless you have lots of extra equipment.

If you're looking for the simplest DAW that's designed with the spoken word in mind, then Hindenburg is worth checking out. But you can shop around for a full range of options at thepodcasthost.com/DAWs

'Podcast Maker' tools

A 'Podcast Maker' is an app or tool that brings everything like recording, editing, production, and publishing together into one place. They can be less flexible and powerful than having a dedicated tool for every job, but so much more simple, convenient, and cost-effective.

Naturally, because we run Alitu, we're a bit biased and think it's the best option out there. We certainly strive to be. But that said, we recognise that there are a few other great options out there too, and we always want to help you make up your own mind.

Podcast hosting giants Podbean, Spreaker, and Anchor each have their own Podcast Maker tools. Their editing and production options can be a bit more limited, but they really shine for those looking to do live shows with real-time audience interaction.

For a deeper look at all the best Podcast Maker options, go to thepodcasthost.com/maker

Why use transcription?

A Podcasting *is* predominantly an audio medium, so, word-for-word episode transcriptions were traditionally seen as a luxury form of bonus content. These days, however, things are different.

Podcasters should *always* be providing transcripts for each new episode they publish. This is for two main reasons.

Firstly - accessibility. Millions of people out there are deaf or hard of hearing. Providing a transcription means that you're not shutting them out from any insights or info on your show that could potentially benefit them.

Secondly - you're keeping yourself on the right side of the law. We've seen recent examples of podcasters facing legal action over their failure to provide transcriptions. It goes without saying that you don't want to risk joining that club.

Transcriptions can be pasted directly into your shownotes, or, you can link clearly to them on a separate page on your site. Some hosting providers even offer dedicated sections where you can publish your transcriptions.

Where to get your podcast transcribed

There are two types of transcription services out there - human, and AI. The AI options are cheaper but generally less accurate, especially if you speak with a Scottish accent. An AI transcription might take a wee bit more time to correct manually, too.

Our podcast-maker tool Alitu now automatically generates transcriptions of all your episodes, so that's one single place you can go to record, edit, publish, and transcribe your show.

Alternatively, if it's human transcription you're after, then our favourite option here is Rev, which you can find at **thepodcasthost.com/rev**

Obviously, with any human service, it'll take up to a few days to get your transcriptions back, whereas AI can do it almost immediately. There's no right or wrong approach here, though. Only what works best for you.

For a deeper dive into podcast transcriptions, with a full range of options, head on over to thepodcasthost.com/transcription

 **Alitu**

AI software

The AI revolution is well underway, and with it, we've seen the emergence of many new tools and software programmes. Some of these are explicitly designed for podcasters, whilst others can be harnessed to streamline podcast workflows and help keep the creative fuel tank topped up.

One such tool that falls into the latter category is ChatGPT. This AI chatbot is frighteningly clever. You can ask it to write anything for you, from a song to an academic paper, and in any style you like, too. For podcasters, this comes in ultra-handy for episode idea generation, future guest suggestions, and even a helping hand in show note writing.

Check out our full guide at thepodcasthost.com/chatgpt for a list of the best prompts you can use when working on your podcast.

There are also AI tools that'll do almost anything else for you, and more are popping up every day. We keep an updated list of them at **thepodcasthost.com/ai.** There, you'll find ways to generate a media kit, marketing materials, or even, an entire podcast episode.

Always remember, though, that AI tools should be there to support your process, but never to do it all for you. The big strength of podcasting is in its human connection. So remember that it's *you* your listeners are turning up to hear from. After all, if they wanted AI-generated content, they could just get it directly from the source!

"Always remember, though, that AI tools should be there to support your process, but never to do it all for you."

Chapter five

Launch & distribution

You've finalised your first episode, now, to get it out into the world! Here's how to publish that show to the web, and get in front of your ideal audience.

In this chapter:
~ How to publish your podcast
~ Where to publish your podcast
~ How to create a podcast trailer
~ Why make an episode zero?
~ Is my podcast "launch" important?
~ Getting listed in podcast directories
~ Getting your show in Apple Podcasts (aka iTunes)
~ Getting your show in Spotify
~ Getting listed in all other podcast directories
~ How to link to and share your podcast

How to publish your podcast

This stage can cause some confusion for new podcasters. You might think you need to upload your episodes to listening platforms like Apple and Spotify, but that isn't the case.

Instead, you create an account with a podcast hosting provider. That's the place your podcast "lives". Your cover art, your show description, and your episodes all go in there. Then, there are a couple of small steps needed to "tell" platforms like Spotify and Apple that your podcast exists.

After that, your show will be listed there, as will each episode you publish within your podcast hosting account. So you only ever need to upload to one single place to have your episodes pushed out to hundreds of listening platforms.

To use an analogy, if your podcast were a magazine, your hosting provider would be the printing press, whilst all of the listening apps and directories would be the shops that your magazine could be found in.

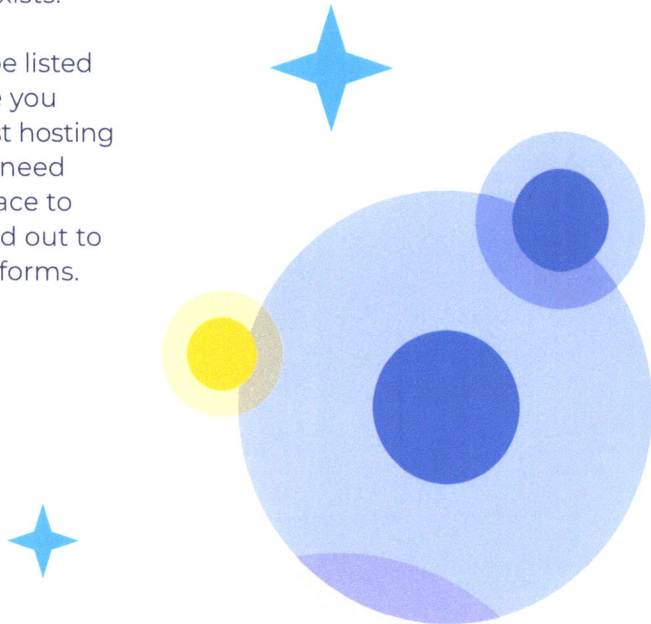

Where to publish your podcast

Your podcast hosting provider - also known as your "podcast host" - is the place you create your show and upload all of your episodes. There are plenty of great hosting options out there catering to all needs and budgets.

Hosting providers will offer you stats so you can see how popular your show is. Some of these go really in-depth and can give you geographic and device stats, too.

Hosting providers will also give you a basic website for your show. Some offer tools for monetisation, growth, and even for creating private "members only" podcasts.

A few of our favourite podcast hosts are Captivate, Transistor, and Castos. You'll find a full rundown of these services and their offerings at **thepodcasthost.com/hosting**

And, our podcast-maker tool Alitu also has hosting included in your subscription. That means you only need one login to record, edit, and publish your podcast, which keeps things cost-effective, and super simple.

How to create a podcast trailer

A promo trailer can help you win over potential new listeners by giving them a flavour of your podcast.

They can easily be played on other shows, too, which can help you grow your audience.

A podcast trailer should be between 30 seconds and a minute. The shorter, the better.

There are things you *definitely* want to mention in your podcast trailer. What's the show called? What's it about? Who is it for? And where can we find it?
If you can add a bit of creative tone, personality, and production, too, then great. But these things are "icing" and shouldn't go in at the expense of the key details.

A podcast trailer is also useful because you need at least one published episode on your feed before you can list your show on places like Spotify and Apple. As far as these platforms are concerned, even a short trailer counts as "an episode".

Another option is to create an episode Zero, which we will look at next.

And, for a deeper dive into creating your trailer, go to thepodcasthost.com/promotrailer

"A podcast trailer should be between 30 seconds and a minute. The shorter, the better."

Why make an episode zero?

This is the name given to a type of introductory or "pre-launch" podcast episode. It isn't *essential* to create an Episode Zero. But many podcasters do – and there are a few good reasons why it might be worth considering for your own show.

An Episode Zero can be similar to a promo trailer in how it introduces your show and your topic. The main difference is length. An Episode Zero would ideally still err on the shorter side of, say, 3-6 minutes. But that still gives you a lot more time than a 30-second trailer.

One of the biggest benefits of an Episode Zero is that it gives you that "one published episode" needed to submit your show everywhere. That means your podcast can be fully set up and ready to go by the time you publish your first "proper" episode.

For a deeper dive on this topic, head on over to thepodcasthost. com/epzero

Is my podcast "Launch" important?

The term "launch" is ambiguous because creating your show and publishing your first episode means you're "launching" your podcast. But we might also think of our launch as something glitzy and hyped-up, like the release of the latest iPhone or Xbox console.

When new tech, or even new books, are released, they only have a few weeks to "sink or swim" because of how sales and charts work in these fields. The good news? This has absolutely nothing in common with podcasting whatsoever.

Some of the most successful podcasters spent months or even years talking to tiny audiences before their consistency and hard work eventually paid off. So, sure, promote and market your new pod as best you can when it's released. But the most important thing isn't how much hype you drum up - it's how soon you get back to work on your next episode!

For a deeper dive into your podcast launch, head on over to thepodcasthost.com/yourlaunch

Getting listed in podcast directories

People listen to podcasts on hundreds of different apps and platforms. In a previous section, we learned that you only need to upload your content to one place - your hosting account - and it'll appear in all these places automatically. But how do we ensure these directories know our podcast exists in the first place?

For this, we use a unique URL called an RSS feed. You'll get one of these when you create your show in your hosting account. You can easily submit this to any directory or app you like. And because Apple Podcasts and Spotify account for about 65% of global podcast listening, you're over halfway there simply by being listed in those two.

And there's more good news. Being listed in Apple Podcasts means you'll automatically be listed in almost all of the other apps and directories out there.

So what initially might've looked like a mammoth task is really just a few minutes of work!

For a deeper dive on this topic, head on over to thepodcasthost. com/directories

65%

of global podcast listening is accounted for through Apple podcasts and Spotify.

Getting your show in apple podcasts (aka iTunes)

Apple has always been - and remains - the number one place podcasts are consumed. We also know that, by being listed here, your show will automatically pop up in a trillion other apps you've never heard of.

To submit to Apple, you just need to create a free Apple ID. Or, you might have one already. Bottom line, you need to log in to **podcastsconnect.apple.com** and click on the 'Add' button. Then, copy and paste your RSS feed from your hosting account, check the details, and submit.

It can take a day or two for your podcast to appear in Apple Podcasts, so don't panic if you don't see it there immediately. Apple will email you if there are any issues, too!

For a deeper dive on submitting to Apple, including screenshots and a video, go to thepodcasthost. com/applepodcasts

Getting your show in Spotify

Spotify is hot on the heels of Apple regarding global podcast consumption. You'll definitely want to get your show listed here. And it's even easier than submitting to their fruit-loving rivals.

Most hosting providers have simple one-click "submit to Spotify" buttons in their distribution sections. What's more, some of our recently launched shows have appeared on Spotify less than an hour after submission.

You can easily submit manually, too, if your host doesn't have a one-click button. Just copy your RSS feed link, go to **podcasters.spotify. com** and paste it to the 'Add a Podcast' section.

The novel thing about the Spotify podcasters portal is that you'll see some data on what music your listeners tend to enjoy. Can you imagine the irony of your death metal podcast throwing up "favourite artists" like The Cheeky Girls and S Club 7? By the way - if that happens to you, please let us know!

And, for a deeper dive on submitting your show to Spotify, go to thepodcasthost.com/ getonspotify

Getting listed in all other podcast directories

As we mentioned before, the fact that you're in Apple Podcasts means you're automatically in a hundred other places. Google Podcasts will start noticing you without you needing to do anything, either - they are in the search business, after all!

But, there are three other platforms you'll want to log in to or create an account for, in order to submit your RSS feed. Those are TuneIn, Amazon, and Audible.

We've got full guides on submitting to each of these platforms, which you can find at thepodcasthost.com/directories

How to link to and share your podcast

This is a big mistake many podcasters make when they promote their content - they share a link to somewhere like Apple or Spotify.

Sure, these places are where a lot of podcast listening happens. But remember, there are hundreds of other apps and directories, too. You definitely can't link to them all, especially not in a tweet, so what do you do?

Quite simply, you send them to one place - your website. We're going to take a deeper dive into making your podcast website in a future section, but you already get a basic webpage as soon as you've signed up for your hosting account. You can even buy a domain name and point it to that webpage whilst you work on setting up something a bit more personalised.

And, for an in-depth look at how to link to your show, head on over to thepodcasthost.com/sharing

Chapter six

Creating
great content

Now that you've conquered the process, let's dig into how to make that content phenomenal! We'll cover a range of content types that are not only compelling to your listeners, but can power growth through sharing, too!

In this chapter:
~ Planning your episodes
~ Coming up with episode ideas
~ Doing question research
~ How to create shareable content
~ The list - creating shareable content
~ The review - creating shareable content
~ The comparison - creating shareable content
~ Costs - creating shareable content
~ Case studies - creating shareable content
~ The how-to - creating shareable content

Planning your episodes

Great podcasters and terrible podcasters have one thing in common - they both make it sound like they haven't planned their episodes.

For the great podcasters, it's because they plan them so well.

For the terrible podcasters, it's because they don't plan them at all.

An episode plan doesn't need to be an in-depth dissertation or treatment. It's more about asking some top-level questions like "Why this topic right now?", "What problem will this solve for my audience?", and "How will this provide value?".

When we cover scripting, we'll talk more about how you bring that plan to the recording booth. But before then, we want to take a look in the next few sections about fleshing out those ideas.

Coming up with episode ideas

As is often the case in podcasting, this depends on your topic. But there are some common themes we see with podcasters coming up with episode ideas.

Maybe a recent personal experience or funny anecdote can tie into your subject or topic. Maybe there's a lesson to be learned from a book you've just read or a movie you've just watched. Or maybe there's something in the news right now that your audience would be interested to hear your take on.

It's a good idea to keep a document of all the evergreen episode ideas you think of, too. That way, you know you've always got something to fall back on if you go through a challenging creative period in the future.

We talked about AI tool ChatGPT in a previous section, and this is an ever-popular method for episode idea generation, too.

To find out more about how you can use it to help inspire your own topics, head on over to thepodcasthost.com/chatgpt

Doing question research

One of the best ways to come up with episode ideas is simply to answer the common questions your audience is asking.

But what if you don't have an audience yet? Well, there are a couple of handy and free ways to find these questions. The first is simply to type something you think your avatar would ask into Google, then scroll down to the bottom, and you'll see suggestions of what they're also asking.

Another is a service called AnswerThePublic.com - here, you just type in your main topic, let's say, "sharks", and it'll spit out every single question people ask about that thing.

From "What do sharks eat?" and "Where sharks are found", to "How sharks sleep" and "Were sharks before dinosaurs?". Your listeners will love these episodes, and they'll throw up some great compelling episode titles, too.

And, once again, it's worth mentioning ChatGPT. With the right prompts, this powerful AI tool will fire out a long list of questions for you to answer on your episodes.

For more on this, head over to thepodcasthost.com/chatgpt

How to create shareable content

Word of mouth is one of the most effective ways to grow your podcast.

According to our 2020 Podcast Discoverability survey, over 33% of listeners find new shows to listen to based on what others have shared or recommended.

So how do you make your podcast episodes shareable, or "recommendable"? There are actually six frameworks you can build your episode around. And, after hearing them, your listeners will be dying to tell others about them, too.

These frameworks are - lists, comparisons, reviews, case studies, how-tos, and costs.

33%

of listeners find new shows to listen to based on what others have shared or recommended.

The list - creating shareable content

Let's face it, we all love lists. There's something compelling about content that promises knowledge like "the top 7 guitarists of all time", or "the best 11 beers in the world right now".

So it's just a case of taking this method and re-working it for your own topic. You can base this on products your listeners might use, places they might visit, recipes they might cook up, or movies they might watch.

Don't get overly hung up on the word "best", too. Just be clear that this is your personal opinion, and that you welcome all feedback and differing viewpoints. The engagement these episodes brings is all part of the fun - and, the wider benefit!

The review - creating shareable content

Before people try or buy things themselves, they generally like to hear the opinions of others. You probably do this yourself each time you nip on to Amazon.

Reviewing products, services, or other topic-relevant things can help your listeners to make more informed decisions.

They'll really appreciate you for this, and they'll want to share these episodes with others each time they see this particular thing being discussed in future, too.

It'll always depend on exactly what you're reviewing, but common points to hit are factors like cost, quality, and ease of use.

So can you write up a list of four or five things you think would make for great review episodes on your own show?

This is another super-shareable type of content, and it can be handy for SEO, too.

The comparison - creating shareable content

Mac versus PC, Pepsi versus Cola, Nike versus Adidas. This is the celebrity death match episode format where you're going to throw two rivals into the arena and see who comes out on top.

Here, you'd tend to look at key relevant factors such as cost, quality, and ease of use. This is almost like the review method, but you're looking at two things, rather than one. We've created these ourselves in the past, where we've had showdowns between popular mics or audio software programmes.

Again, this is totally topic dependent. Do you podcast about mountain biking? Well, let's hear your take on the two most popular brands of tyres. Or, are you more of a business coach? Then maybe your listeners would like your help deciding on one of two popular types of accounting software.

There will almost definitely be opportunities for comparisons within your niche, so have a think about what initial episodes you can plan out.

Costs - creating shareable content

When people buy things these days, they do their research online first. So here's where you can help your target audience get the info they need.

What cost-related questions do you think they might commonly type into Google?

For example, a nutritional therapy podcast might run an episode titled "How much does a food intolerance test cost?".

Or a show about living off-grid might run one about, "How much does a wood-burning stove cost?".

You might even do a cost list where you compare your own product or service to your competitors. This honest approach can help build trust and authority, too.

Case studies - creating shareable content

Case studies use examples of people doing things, or events taking place. For example, a biking podcast might do a deep dive into how one rider prepared for and won a big tournament.

Or a football podcast might chronicle the journey of a team of underdogs from a small village who won a national trophy.

You can almost think of it as a movie. It's a great opportunity to tell a story - and stories are the ultimate and oldest form of shareable content.

Try to answer questions like "What's their main motivation?", "what are their biggest obstacles?", and "What are they doing differently?". This will leave your listener feeling clued up, motivated, and inspired!

The how-to - creating shareable content

This is the classic problem-solution pairing.
What is your audience struggling with?
What do they need help with?

You might already have a decent idea of this, based on our recent 'Question Research' section.

Starting your title with, "How to" is arguably the most effective way of getting folks to click on it. You might say, "Well, that's just clickbait". But is it really "just clickbait" if it delivers what it promises?

Some examples of 'how-to' episodes that'll have their target audience hitting play without a second thought are:

· 'How to become a scratch golfer'
· 'How to improve your sleep quality'
· 'How to talk to your kids about grief'
· And, 'How to pass your driving test'

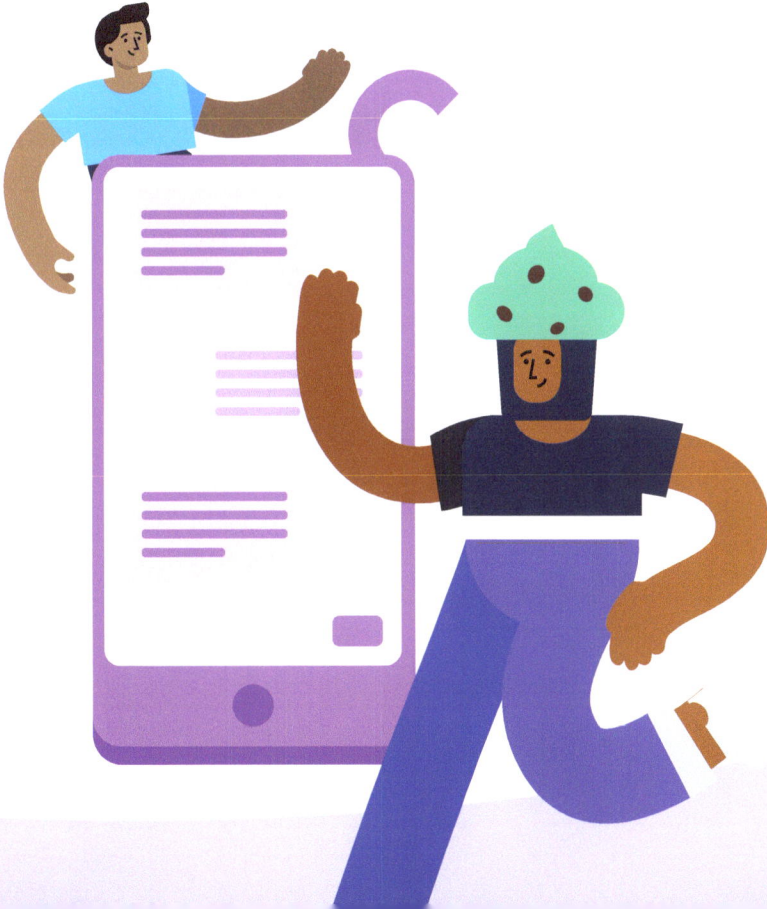

Chapter seven

Scripts, hooks, & CTAs

When you're in the day-to-day of podcasting, the script is your core tool. Let's look at how to script your show, what to include in the recurring intros and outros, and how to make sure you're powering audience growth.

In this chapter:
~ Writing a podcast script
~ Word-for-word podcast scripts
~ Detailed podcast scripts
~ Rough podcast scripts
~ Introducing & ending your episodes
~ What to include in your episode intros
~ Hooking your listener early
~ Using cold opens
~ What makes a good podcast outro?
~ What to include in your episode outro

Writing a podcast script

Podcast scripting is a very personal thing. Some hosts script their whole show, word for word. Other hosts write down the episode title and just ad-lib it from there. Neither way is right nor wrong, and, in reality, most people go for something in-between.

Scripting can be viewed as a spectrum, with fully-scripted and not-even-slightly-scripted covering each end.

That means it's impossible to tell you exactly how to do it. But, we can tell you a *few ways* to do it.

You can try each way out, and tweak them for your needs. With a bit of trial and error, you'll find the type of scripting that best suits you.

Word-for-word podcast scripts

This method is great because you'll never forget or leave anything out. It can also help a lot if you lack the confidence to speak for any length of time.

But, there are big cons, too. Scripting a show this way takes ages. Few podcasters can also pull off word-for-word reading and make it sound conversational. You run the risk of your episodes being a bit flat and monotone.

By all means, give it a shot. But it will unlikely be the best option for you in the long run.

Detailed podcast scripts

This is the most common way of scripting a podcast. It's a great alternative to the word-for-word method. Here, you can write down every point you want to hit, every resource you want to mention, and every story you want to cover.

You're not trying to script every single word, though, so you still have that freedom to talk naturally *with* your listener, instead of reading *at* them. Your personality can shine through here, without the risk of going off-track or forgetting something.

Rough podcast scripts

This one is near the 'make-it-up-as-you-go-along' end of the scripting spectrum

Here, you'll mainly use bullet points to remind you where you're going. You're relying on your expert knowledge of the subject to fill in the gaps.

This leads to the most conversational type of podcast and is often the most engaging. When you're speaking from experience, your voice becomes a lot more active, and a lot less monotone.

The problem, of course, is that there's a chance that you'll miss stuff or maybe even get something wrong. So the time you might've saved in doing a more detailed script can easily be spent on extra editing or re-recording.

For an in-depth look at podcast scripting, go to thepodcasthost.com/scripting

Introducing & ending your episodes

Obviously, the most important part of any podcast episode is its main content. But how you open and close your episodes is vital for listeners even getting to that stage.

Think about it, each episode you release will be someone's first impression of your show. On top of that, you only have five minutes to "hook" a third of all podcast listeners. That's according to recent data from our Podcast Discoverability survey.

So you need to leave them with absolutely no doubt that this episode is a must-listen. Then, after you've delivered on your promise, you need to finish strongly enough that they'll return for more.

What to include in your episode intros

There are few "rules" in podcasting - it's a creative medium, after all. With that said, you can really optimise the intro of your episodes if you include the following things.

Firstly, let the listener know who they're talking to. So, whether you go by your real name or a nickname - introduce yourself.

Next, - the title of the show. You might assume they already know it. But they may be working through a huge playlist of new podcasts they're trying out.

Then, crucially, tell them who it's for and what's in it for them. So, the overall podcast topic might be "to learn Spanish", and the subject of this episode might be "ordering at a restaurant". This is all part of your "hook".

Hooking your listener early

Podcast listeners are selfish. I don't mean that in a bad way. It's just that everyone tunes into content with one question in mind - "What's in this for me?".

If anything is drawn out, confusing, or ambiguous, it's easy for them to lose interest and switch off.

You always have creative freedom with your podcast. But here's a template you can use as a starting point.

"Hello and welcome to the *blank* Podcast. This is the show for *blank*, all about *blank*, and on this episode, have you ever struggled with *blank*?

Well, that's exactly what we're going to help you with on this week's show, where you'll learn how to *blank*"

Your target listener hears this and thinks, "This is exactly what I've been looking for". And then, all you need to do is deliver on your promise...

Using cold opens

You know when you sit down to watch your favourite TV show and the episode starts before you've even opened your bag of Doritos? Then, after about five minutes, the intro kicks in? Well, that's what's known as a "cold open".

Many podcasters use cold opens at the beginning of their episodes. You've probably heard them before. You hit play, and immediately seem to have landed bang in the middle of a guest explaining, "...so it was at this point I decided to wear a diving suit made of sirloin steaks and go swimming with sharks."

Obviously, the idea is that you think "wait, how is this idiot still alive to tell the tale? I need to get the full story." And you keep on listening. Cold opens can be a compelling way to hook listeners.

"Cold opens can be a compelling way to hook listeners."

What makes a good podcast outro?

The final minute or two of your episode goes towards creating a lasting impression in the mind of your listener.

You might have done a great job with the intro and main content. But if the show ends poorly, this can be the difference between a new listener hitting 'follow' or not.

The job of the outro is essentially to thank the listener for their time. Then, point them in the direction of any vital resources mentioned in the episode.

It's also the part where you can ask for something in return. If a listener has stayed to the end, they've probably enjoyed the episode, so they might be more willing to respond to your request for something like a rating, review, or even a sale.

What to include in your episode outro

Just like the podcast intro, there are no "rules" as such, but if you want to close your episode effectively, think about the following.

Send them to ONE place - your website. Here they can find show notes with links to everything mentioned in the episode. Put transcriptions and follow-up resources here, too.

Next, include ONE 'Call to Action' - for example, "follow or subscribe to the podcast". If you give them too much to do, chances are, they won't do any of it. Other CTA options might be things like "tell a friend", "buy the book", or "support the show".

Finally, if possible, offer them a teaser for the next episode. Whet their appetite for what's in store, and keep your show fresh in their mind until a new one drops.

For a deeper dive on this topic, head over to thepodcasthost. com/outros

Chapter eight

Being great in front of the mic

With a plan in place, it's time to get in front of the mic. But how do we make sure we're sharing our best selves? Here are a set of tips and tactics to get the best from your voice and be comfortable on the mic.

In this chapter
~ Pre-recording practicalities
~ What should I drink before or during recording?
~ Should I eat before recording?
~ Minimising recording interruptions
~ Mic technique
~ What if I make a mistake when recording?

Pre-recording practicalities

This is the less glamorous but still vitally important side of recording. Your gear and environment aren't the only factors determining whether you sound like a seasoned pro or a complete beginner.

As the old saying goes - "failing to prepare is preparing to fail".

Or, here's a good one to test your mic's pop filter - "prior preparation prevents poor performance."

In the next few sections, we'll take a look at things like mic technique, minimising interruptions, and even how what you eat or drink can affect your show's audio quality.

"Failing to prepare is preparing to fail".

What should I drink before or during recording?

Getting behind the mic whilst dehydrated is a bad idea for several reasons. Firstly, you're just going to have less energy and feel a bit groggy.

Secondly, you'll make more dry lip-smacking mouth noises that'll have your listener reaching for the 'unfollow' button.

So be sure to have some water before and during your session. Don't go overboard, though, as overhydration can lead to excessive mouth noises, too. Plus, There's nothing worse than needing a pee ten minutes into an engaging interview.

For some podcasters, coffee is their superpower. For others, it can really dry out their mouths. Only you'll know best what camp you fall into here.

In summary, though, a moderate amount of water before and during recording works best for most podcasters.

But, for a deeper dive on this topic, head on over to thepodcasthost.com/drink

Should I eat before recording?

It's worth saying right away, that, unless you run an ASMR podcast, you probably want to avoid eating *during* a recording session.

Some podcasters feel they have more energy if they're in a bit of a fasted state when they get behind the mic. Others will snack beforehand on foods that aren't likely to dry out their mouth or cause brain fog.

Many voice coaches swear by green apples for hydrating the mouth. Some other podcasters we know use liquorice to soothe their throats.

Nuts and seeds also make for useful pre-recording snacks, whilst common things to avoid are dairy, overly-salty foods, and refined sugars.

But, you should always get to know your own body and your own reaction to foods. Everyone's different, after all. So only ever do what works best for you.

And, for a deeper dive on this topic, head on over to thepodcasthost.com/food

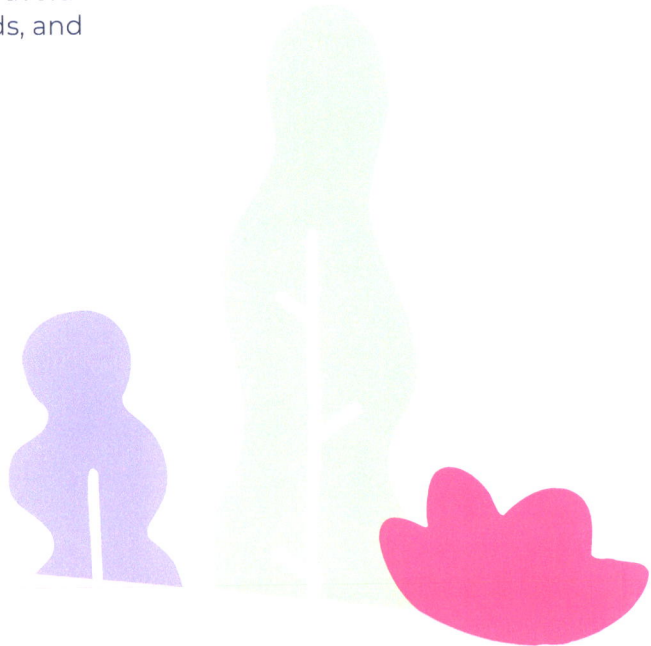

Minimising recording interruptions

These are the low-hanging fruits of making your podcast easier to edit, sound better, and generally cause you less frustration.

To deal with the digital side of things, you should close any apps that will ping or distract you when you're recording. (I'm looking at you, Slack!)

Then, it's worth telling anyone you live with that you're going to be recording for the next hour or so. An extreme measure might be a "do not disturb" sign on your door, but most people will only need a quick heads-up.

Finally, get that phone on silent and keep it away from you during the show. These are three quick and simple tips, but they really can make a world of difference.

For a deeper dive on this topic, head over to thepodcasthost.com/noise

Mic technique

It's not the size or the shape that matters, but how you use it. I'm talking, of course, about mic technique.

The optimal positioning of a mic depends on your own unique voice and style. A good starting point, though, is the distance between the tips of your thumb and pinkie on an outstretched hand. Then, adjust accordingly.

Always try to mount your mic in a stand or boom arm, rather than holding it. This will give you a lot more consistency of sound, and prevent unwanted handling noise.

Finally, use a windshield or pop filter on your mic, especially if you prefer to get right up close to it when talking.

Using your mic well in a treated environment means you'll get good audio even with the most low-cost setup. So follow these quick steps, and your podcast will sound much more professional.

For a deeper dive into this topic, head over to thepodcasthost.com/mictechnique

What if I make a mistake when recording?

Stumbles and stammers are natural. But, if you always stop and start again, thinking, "I'll just edit that out", then your podcast is going to become time-consuming or expensive to create. With minor mistakes, just quickly correct yourself, make light of it, and press on.

Of course, there are times when you'll want to get something spot on. Maybe you're presenting a fact, or making a very serious point. When you make a mistake here, just pause, click your fingers three times in front of the mic, and then start again.

If you do this, you'll quickly and easily spot essential edit points in the production phase. And as for the minor stuff, just let it go. You'll grow into a much more accomplished presenter over time this way, as opposed to the folks who use editing as a crutch in an attempt to make them sound flawless.

For a deeper dive on this topic, head to thepodcasthost.com/editfaster

Chapter nine

Interviews & guests

A commonly underestimated skill, but a core tool in any podcaster's arsenal, interviewing is something that you can hone and master over time. Let's look at the process, from finding guests to getting the best from them.

In this chapter:

Organising guests or co-hosts

If you think tech and equipment can be challenging, then you should try wrangling humans.

Your guests or co-hosts could live in any time zones around the globe. They might be super-organised, but they might also be pretty shambolic, easily distracted, and forgetful.

Then, there are the conversations themselves. How do you make people sound their best on your show? Even if they're giving you little more than one-word answers. OR, aren't letting you get a word in edgeways?

In the next few sections, we'll give you some essential tips on organising and talking to your guests and co-hosts.

"How do you make people sound their best on your show?"

Finding podcast guests

If you run an interview podcast, it can be challenging to get folks to come on your show at first.

A great starting point is to approach other podcasters in your niche. They already know how it all works, and you know they'll sound great, too. On top of that, if they share the episode with their own audience, it's going to send some early traffic your way.

Then, there are YouTubers, bloggers, or authors who're typically always up for a chat, too. There are even dedicated services to help you find interviewees. Or even, to get booked as a guest on other shows. Check out Podchaser Connect, PodcastGuests.com, or Matchmaker FM for three of our favourites. And it's worth mentioning that you can also use AI tool ChatGPT to come up with a list of potential guests for your podcast.

Or, get our full guide to this topic, including links to the sites mentioned here, head on over to thepodcasthost.com/guests

Booking tools for guests or co-hosts

Different time zones, and scheduling conflicts can drop you into an endless cycle of messages where days and times are suggested but never agreed upon.

If you're regularly trying to arrange suitable dates and times with others, it's well worth using a tool like Calendly or Book Like a Boss. These platforms can show folks all the times you're available, and they simply need to pick a slot that suits them.

Another great tool is Doodle which comes in handy for organising groups of three or more. A Doodle poll lets people pick all their available times, and then you'll see - at a glance - the ones that everyone can manage.

Again, those three tools are Doodle, Calendly, and Book Like a Boss.

For a deeper dive on this topic, and links to the platforms mentioned, head on over to thepodcasthost.com/booking

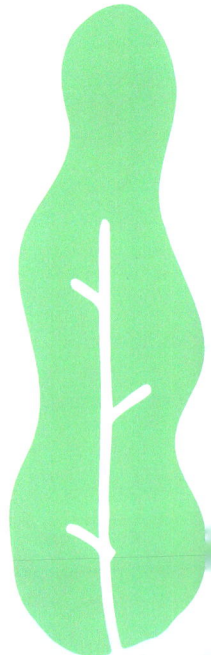

Why is this guest on my show?

Now that might sound a little rude, but don't worry, this is the question we ask ourselves *before* we even invite someone onto our podcast.

In order to answer this question, you need to put yourself in the shoes... or earbuds... of your audience. Ask yourself, "What value can this person bring to my listener?" Will they teach them something? Motivate them? Make them laugh?

Your listener's attention is precious, and you're one of the few people they trust with it. So once you know *why* you're bringing a person onto your show, you can prepare properly to ensure they get the maximum value from that time.

Everyone wins here - your audience enjoys it, your guest sounds great, and your show has its desired impact, which helps it to grow.

Introducing podcast guests

It's those dreaded words "so, tell us a bit about yourself" that can lead to you waking up, six hours later, listening to an interviewee ramble on about his toy car collection.

This isn't the guest's fault. They've just been handed the mic and let off the leash with no real direction. They don't know your audience.

But you do.

And it's your job to succinctly introduce your guest to them with a quick rundown of who they are, and *why they're here*.

Remember we talked about the value your guest will bring? Well, let your listener know that as soon as possible. Keep them engaged and tuned in.

Sure, there's room to explore personal and off-topic stuff, but that should be done towards the end - after you've given your listener the content they've been promised.

Asking follow-up questions

So, your guest just finished telling you they built a time machine, travelled back 70 million years, and shot a T-Rex.

You take a look at your next question and ask, "So, what's your favourite WordPress plugin?".

Interviewers who *actually* listen to their guests and ask good follow-up questions often find the real gold.

Questions like "What was that like?"

"Why do you think that?"

Or, "Could you explain what this means?" can lead you to some fantastic content.

Sure, have a list of pre-written questions. But use these as a framework or backup if things fall flat.

Always pick up on threads that seem interesting or curious. Even if you know the answer, your listener might not. And you're here to bring value to them, not to make them feel dumb, left out, or wanting more.

Should I send questions in advance?

You'll probably have a list of pre-written questions as a framework for your interviews. But as we've covered already, you won't want to ask these in a linear 'game show host' style.

On top of that, sending a guest a list of questions in advance can cause them to overthink and rehearse answers. This doesn't make for a very engaging or authentic conversation.

Certain questions *are* worth pre-warning about, though. These are what's known as "thinkers". An example might be something like "What's your favourite book?" or "What advice do you have for someone just starting out?". It's unlikely anyone can give genuine answers to questions like these on the spot, so they're definitely worth a heads-up in advance. But - these are the exception to the rule.

Seek out stories in your interviews

As we've mentioned before, stories are the original and best type of shareable content.

There's a subtle but powerful difference between "Here's how to grow a business" and "Here's how *I* grew *my* business".

Stories are never just straightforward routes to success either. They're littered with setbacks, conflicts, emotions, and seemingly "all is lost" moments.

Your listener wants to live through these with you and learn from the experiences, not just the end product. It's worth asking your guest if they have any interesting or entertaining stories before you hit the record button, too. Don't let

them actually tell you the story there and then. All you need is a heads-up so you can prompt them about it during their interview, and then, introduce it naturally.

For a deeper dive into this topic, head on over to thepodcasthost. com/interviewprep

"Stories are the original and best type of shareable content."

Asking core questions about the guest

This is another wing to your storytelling angle. It lets the listener focus on the guest themselves. People love to hear things in context, after all.

"Believe in yourself and never give up!" is all well and good. But people often can't see that applying to them... until they hear a story about it happening to someone else.

Here are some examples of questions that can lead to engaging and insightful podcast interviews:

- Which hurdles did you personally face, and how did you overcome them?
- Was it obvious, or did you stumble upon the answers?
- How did you get started? Talk me through it.
- What compelled you to become a screenwriter?

Again, this gives your listener a peek behind the curtain and shows them that the guest was once in a similar position as they are now. And what could be more encouraging than that?

Asking core questions about the topic

Here, we can dig in and explore by asking your guest some seemingly provocative questions. They'll usually be glad to answer these as it gives them a chance to counter claims they'll hear a lot.

"So, you're a Vegan Baking Specialist – isn't it really hard to bake without eggs?"

Or

"Doesn't homeschooling just deprive kids of making friends?"

With these types of questions, you can pick out some common myths or misconceptions to talk through and clarify.

You might also want to ask a question like "What's the most common reason people fail at this?", which sounds negative, but can throw up some really actionable answers.

Then there's the classic "What's the one thing you wish you knew when you were just getting started?" which puts a much better spin on the old "advice for folks just starting out" question.

Super podcast interview questions

When you cover the basics well, you can go the extra mile to help make your guest stand out from everyone else. Here are some fun questions that can entertain your listener whilst still leaving them with a few useful insights, too:

- What are you NOT Very Good at?
- Tell me something that's true that almost nobody agrees with you on.
- When did you last change your mind about something?
- Room, desk and car – which do you clean first?
- What's the very first thing you think about when you wake up in the morning?

These questions allow for that essential human touch. They can throw up humility, authenticity, wisdom, and even, a wee bit of controversy.

They'll leave a lasting impression in the minds of your listeners, and that's ultimately what gets them sharing your content, and keeps them coming back for more.

For a deeper dive into this topic, head on over to thepodcasthost.com/questions

Encouraging guests to share your episodes

Whether we like it or not, no guest is obliged to share your content with their audience. But if you follow the advice in the previous sections, your chat should be memorable enough to make them want to.

The key is to ask nicely, and to make it easy for them. Be sure to succinctly remind them why you think the conversation will be interesting and valuable to *their* audience.

Some podcasters even pre-write a social media post, so all the groundwork is done for them.

If you go the extra mile and create some nice blog and social graphics around the interview, that's going to make it more shareable, too. Oh, and one final tip - why not have some branded podcast swag sent over to them via a service like GuestBoxLove?

For a deeper dive into this topic, head on over to thepodcasthost. com/guestsharing

Chapter ten

Podcast music

Music can provide polish to your show, and build a really recognizable audio brand over time. But how do you find a good tune, and make sure it's legal for you to use? Here is a range of tips to put some musicality into your show!

In this chapter:
~ Do I need podcast music?
~ Can I use any music in my podcast?
~ So, what music can I use in my podcast?
~ Where to find free podcast music
~ Where to buy podcast music

Do I need podcast music?

There's no rule to say that your show *must* have music. But many podcasters stick some at the beginning and end of the show to add that extra layer of production, professionalism, and identity.

Just be wary of letting music play on its own for any longer than ten seconds on your podcast. Whilst TV and film can get away with this because of their visual elements, it doesn't work that way in audio. Your listeners are plugging in to hear from you - not an extended version of your theme tune.

You can also use music as transitions in-between segments, or as "beds" underneath speech. For most podcasters, though, this is overkill, and you risk annoying your listener rather than impressing them.

Can I use ANY music in my podcast?

The short answer here is "no". And any music you hear on the radio or your favourite Spotify playlist is probably off-limits.

Be wary of myths like "It's fine if it's less than seven seconds" and "It's okay so long as you're not making money with your podcast".

"Fair Use" gets quoted a lot, too. Fair use is a defence you can use if you get in trouble. But who wants to get in trouble?

In short, avoid this altogether. Your podcast isn't going to live or die based on whether you have Bohemian Rhapsody as your theme tune. And if it does, then you likely need to get back to the content planning stages.

For a deeper dive on this topic, head on over to thepodcasthost. com/copyright

So, what music CAN I use in my podcast?

Whilst Harry Styles' latest track is strictly off-limits, there are plenty of music options that are safe, legal, and - in some cases - free to use on your podcast.

Two terms you'll often come across are "Creative Commons" and "Royalty-Free". Creative Commons usually means you can use music for free, so long as you credit and link back to the creator.

Royalty-Free, on the other hand, usually means that you've paid up-front for a license to use a piece of music, going forward.

There are variations on Creative Commons and Royalty-Free licenses - for example, commercial and non-commercial - so our definitions shouldn't be considered blanket terms. In the next couple of sections, we'll point you towards some resources for actually finding music for your show.

In the meantime, though, be sure to check out our full guide at thepodcasthost.com/music

Where to find free podcast music

There's no shortage of tracks out there that you can use 100% free of charge, so long as you credit and link back to the creator in your show notes.

We run a free podcast music library ourselves, and you're totally welcome to pick something from there. Head on over to **thepodcasthost.com/freemusic** for a look.

Incompetech.com is probably the most famous creative commons music resource on the web, too. There's a lot of fantastic material available over there.

The big downside of free music is that many other podcasters use the same tracks. It can be hard to build a memorable brand if your theme tune pops up repeatedly on countless other shows.

Where to buy podcast music

You *can* buy song licenses outright. But the most common route is to pay a monthly subscription for a service where you can use anything on there for the duration of that subscription. These libraries usually include sound effects, too.

Many services grant you a lifetime license here, so you don't need to go back and remove music from previous episodes after you've cancelled your subscription, and there are rarely download limits, either. Obviously, you should always check the terms and conditions of any platform you decide to use, though.

Two of our favourite places to buy podcast music are Epidemic and Shutterstock. If you head on over to **thepodcasthost.com/music** we regularly have coupon code deals for them, too.

In that guide, you'll also find a link to Music Radio Creative, which is another great service that can produce premium quality voice-branded intros and outros for your show.

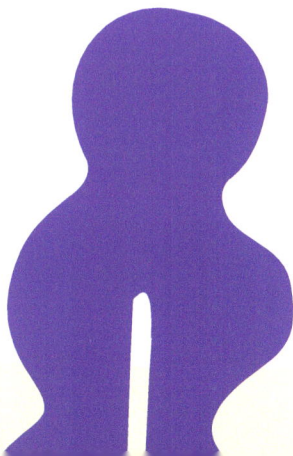

In this chapter:
~ Editing & producing your podcast
~ How much editing should I do?
~ Minimum effective podcast editing
~ Noise reduction & audio clean-up
~ What is compression?
~ How loud should a podcast be?

Chapter eleven

Editing & production

One of the most commonly voiced frustrations in podcasting is editing, and it can eat up a lot of time if you let it. Let's look at how to develop the right mindset around editing so that it doesn't become a terrible time-suck and slowly kill your show.

Editing & producing your podcast

This is the phase of podcasting where you chop out all your mistakes and cut the fat from your conversations. You can also clean up your audio to remove any background hiss and level it to make everything consistently loud enough.

Then, you can mix in things like music, transitions, and pre-recorded segments.

Naturally, this is the part of podcasting that puts tonnes of people off. Very few folks have ever used audio editing software, which is often complex and designed predominantly for musicians.

But, as we found out earlier in our software sections, there are options out there for all experience levels. So once you've picked your weapon of choice, it's time to think about actually doing the work at hand.

How much editing should I do?

As is often the case in podcasting, the answer is "It depends". As we've covered before, there are loads of different types of podcasts. So a one-minute scripted solo show will need much less editing than a two-hour documentary-style epic.

Unless you enjoy editing - and most podcasters don't - you just need to do enough to make your show sound good. And then, leave it at that.

Two big keys to podcasting success are consistency and sustainability. So if you find yourself spending a tonne of time bogged down in your editing software, chances are, you're not going to enjoy it. It won't be long before you convince yourself there are better things to do.

So, how do you strike that balance between "enough" and "not too much"? That's where Minimum Effective Podcast Editing comes in.

> **"Two big keys to podcasting success are consistency and sustainability."**

Minimum effective podcast editing

Remember we talked about making mistakes during recording? Our tip was to pause, click your fingers three times into the mic, and then start again.

Well, now you have a quick and easy way to spot anything that needs chopping out.

Aside from that, you'll want to "top and tail" your recording, cutting any preamble at the start and drawn-out goodbyes at the end.

Then it's the cleanup and volume levelling stuff, which you can either learn to do in a DAW. Or, have a 'Podcast Maker' tool like Alitu take care of that for you, automatically.

Piece together any segments, music, or other clips in your editing software or Alitu's episode builder, and you'll be ready to export and publish.

Podcast editing doesn't need to be a slog, especially with the right planning, processes, and tools at your disposal.

For a deeper dive into our minimum effective editing approach, head on over to thepodcasthost.com/mee

Noise reduction & audio clean-up

Some types of background noise can be cleaned up in the post-production phase. The constant hiss of a fan, or the low static hum of a microphone, for example. Audio software has the ability to recognise this and strip it out, whilst leaving the vocals intact.

Of course, it's easy to go overboard with this and ruin the vocals themselves. Working with noise reduction is a bit like walking a tightrope. Or, using magic in a high fantasy novel.

We can teach you how to do it, free with Audacity, at **thepodcasthost. com/audacitynoise**. Or, if you're using Alitu, it's all done for you automatically, so you don't need to know a single thing about it.

One final note on background noise - the environmental stuff like phones ringing and dogs barking isn't going to be removed by standard noise reduction processes. So always make sure you're recording the best possible source material.

Noise reduction can help good audio to sound great, but it can never make terrible audio sound good.

For a deeper dive into this topic, head to thepodcasthost.com/ noise

What is compression?

No, this isn't about blowing your car tyres up. Compression is an audio production technique where you take the loudest and quietest bits of a conversation, and bring them closer together. It's all about achieving volume-level consistency.

Compression allows you to have loud laughter and soft whispering in your episode, and, if done well, your listener won't need to adjust the volume dial.

Just like noise reduction, compression needs a subtle touch, though, and it's easy to go overboard. We can teach you how to do it, free with Audacity, at **thepodcasthost.com/ audacitycompressor**

Or, once again, you can simply have Alitu do it all for you automatically without needing to know the slightest thing about how it works.

How loud should a podcast be?

We've talked about having consistent volume levels throughout your episodes. But what about the overall volume level of your show compared to other podcasts?

Audio loudness is measured in something called "LUFS", which means "Loudness Units relative to Full Scale". Sounds exciting, eh?

Recommended podcast loudness varies, depending on who you ask, and whether your episode is mono or stereo. But a good ballpark to aim for is between -16 and -21 LUFS.

You can set this process up in a DAW like Adobe Audition. Or, it's yet another factor that Alitu takes care of for you automatically, without you knowing anything about it. Regardless of how you get there, your listeners will be grateful when they land on your episode after listening to another show, because it won't blow their eardrums out or make them think their earbuds have run out of battery.

For a deeper dive into this topic, head on over to thepodcasthost. com/loudness

What's the difference between a WAV and an MP3?

The major difference between WAVs and MP3s are size and quality. WAV files contain more detail but are also much bigger. Think of a WAV file as an original painting and MP3 files as prints of that painting.

Podcast episodes are almost always released in MP3 form because it has a good file size-to-quality ratio. MP3s have their own size and quality scale too. They're called bitrates, and we will discuss them in the next section.

WAVs are known as a "lossless" format because they contain the full detail of the original recording.

But only a handful of people in the world could listen to spoken-word content in its WAV form, and on a good MP3 version of it, and be able to tell the difference.

MP3s keep storage and cost down for you and your listeners. And you won't be shocked to learn that Alitu exports your episodes in MP3 form for you, automatically.

What Are Bitrates in MP3s?

Bitrates represent a sliding scale of quality and size regarding the MP3 file format. They're measured in kbps, or, kilobits per second.

Common bitrates for music files are 128 and 192kbps. As most podcasts are purely spoken-word content we probably don't need to go this high, though.

With our own shows, we tend to opt for 96kbps, but some go as low as 64kbps - most famously, Marc Maron. And he does alright, eh?

If setting your bitrates manually, you'll also need to choose between Constant Bitrate and Variable

Bitrate. For podcasting, you should always choose "Constant".

These are options you'll find in any DAW when you're exporting your episode to MP3 form. And, surprise, surprise, your pal Alitu just gets on with it and does it all for you.

For a deeper dive into this topic, head on over to thepodcasthost. com/bitrates

What are Hz and sample rates?

Sample rates are measured in hertz, or "Hz". Like bitrates, sample rates in audio determine audio quality and file size. You could compare them to pixels in a photograph.

Some platforms and tools will ask you to set a sample rate before hitting record. The most common sample rate, which we'd recommend, is 44,100Hz.

If you load up your audio in your DAW and zoom right in as far as possible, you'd see your audio represented as little dots. The more dots per second, the higher the sample rate. Again, these are just like pixels.

So next time you record in your DAW, choose 44,100Hz. Or, just use Alitu, and yet again, you won't need to worry about this.

For a deeper dive into this topic, head on over to thepodcasthost. com/samplerates

What is bit depth?

So each audio sample – those little dots in your waveform – has a 'bit depth', which determines the quality of the sound.

Some tools will ask you to select a bit depth before recording. The most common bit depths are 16, 24, and 32.

As is often the case, the higher the number, the higher the quality.

Higher bit depths are better at handling noise, with substantial differences between their quietest and loudest parts.

But this is much more relevant to musicians than to those recording the spoken word.

So if you're asked, just opt for 16, and set your levels so nobody is at risk of peaking or clipping. Bit depth is yet another thing Alitu handles behind the scenes, too. At this rate, it will be making you a cup of coffee and a sandwich, eh?

Chapter twelve

Your podcast website

To grow well, you need a great home base for your podcast. Here we look at the different ways to create one, and what to include in it to engage listeners, and grow your audience.

In this chapter:
~ Do I need a podcast website?
~ Wordpress podcast websites
~ Podpage podcast websites
~ Domain names
~ Podcast episode pages
~ Podcast episode show notes
~ Creating an 'about' page
~ Creating a 'subscribe' or 'follow' page
~ Creating a list of podcast episodes
~ Sharing buttons
~ Creating a 'start here' page
~ The end? far from it!

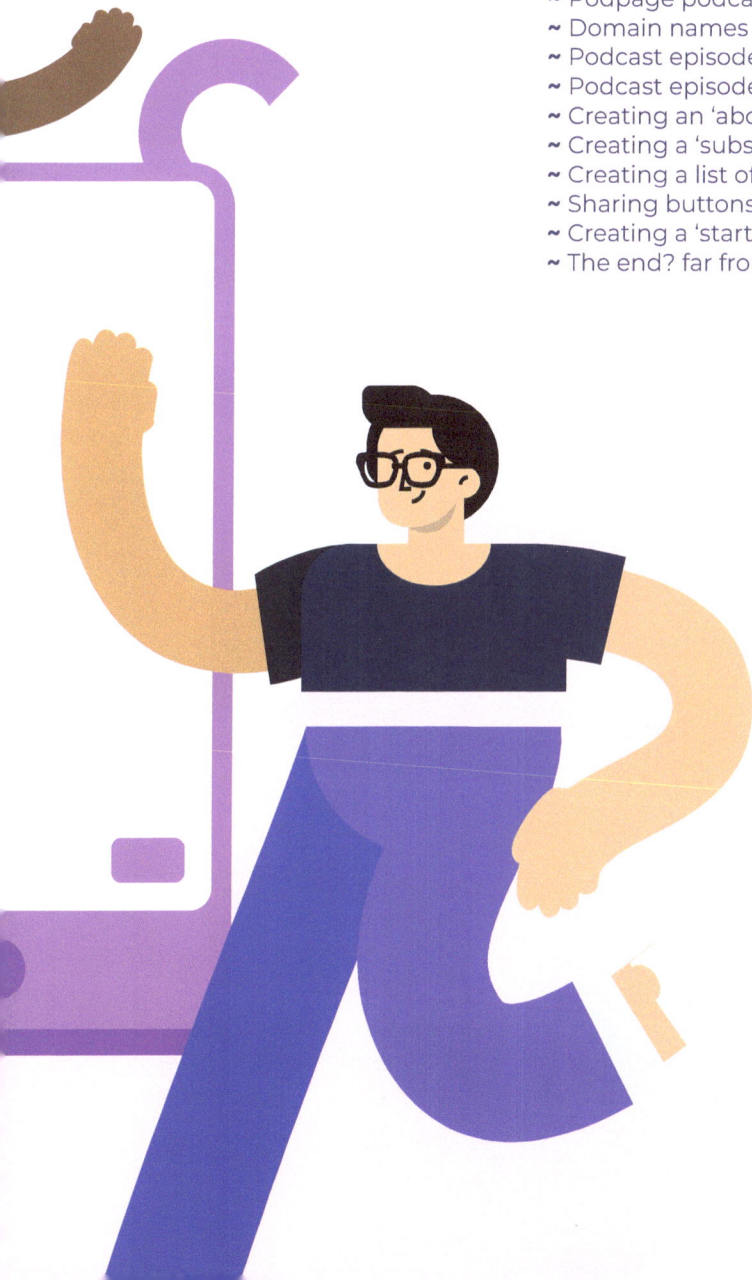

Do I need a podcast website?

The short answer here is "no". You don't *need* a website for your podcast. But the benefits of having one are almost too good to ignore.

For starters, just having that one central place to send people means your podcast is much more shareable. We already know that podcast listening happens on a multitude of different apps, so it simplifies things when you can just say, "Find us on my podcast dot com", or whatever the URL is.

Running your own website then means you have full control over your branding, and if you plan to sell products or services in the future, too, then this is going to give you a massive head start.

Your hosting provider does create a basic website for you by default. Some of these are actually pretty decent, and getting better all the time. However, there are a couple of options that can help you take it to the next level, and we're going to cover them in the next two sections.

WordPress podcast websites

If you're looking for 100% full control, ownership, and customisation options, then WordPress is for you. Here, you can use all sorts of plugins and tools to make your site do pretty much anything. You can run your entire business there.

However, all of this flexibility comes at a cost. There are always things that can break or go wrong. If you don't have the expertise to run a site like this, then you'll need to hire someone who does. There's nothing worse than waking up in the morning to see that your site has gone down overnight.

So, is there a middle ground between a fully-fledged WordPress site and the default website given to you as part of your podcasting hosting account? Actually, yes...

Podpage podcast websites

Podpage is a service that can build you a website for your show in less than five minutes. And you don't need to know the slightest thing about web design, either.

You can use Podpage for free, but their paid tiers offer a whole suite of additional tools for SEO, community, and monetisation.

To give you a hint of the types of features at your disposal, you can keep track of ratings and reviews, get listener comments and voicemails, build a mailing list, offer memberships, and track analytics.

Sure, Podpage is a third-party service, so you don't have that 100% control and ownership as you would with a WordPress site. But for most podcasters, the pros far outweigh the cons here. And there's actually very little you can't do with a Podpage site.

For a full review of the service, head on over to thepodcasthost. com/podpagereview

Domain names

Whether you're using a default hosting provider website, a Podpage site, or a self-hosted WordPress site, you can buy and use a domain name.

Domain names are, most famously, dot coms. But you can buy local variations, dot nets, or dot pretty much anything else these days.

Whatever you choose, just try to make it memorable, easy to read out, and most of all, easy to type in. Avoid things like hyphens in your domain name, for example.

If you've got your heart set on one that will be tricky to punch in, then you might want to buy a few variations of it and point those to your site, too.

An example of this might be a domain name with a number in it. You'd buy one version with the number, and another version with the number spelt out. But do try your best to avoid these situations in the first place.

Podcast episode pages

It's good practice to create a page or blog post for each podcast episode you release. This gives you one handy place to share each episode, and it means all of the traffic is coming to your own platform, too.

Here, the title of your episode would also be the title of your page or post. You'd embed the episode player, preferably near the top. Whilst most folks don't listen to full episodes this way, it's good to give them a taster and point them off to a few dedicated podcast listening platforms in the process.

You'd also add in your shownotes, containing links to anything mentioned in that episode. And you can add some episode-specific graphics or images to these pages, too.

Podcast episode show notes

Show notes are basically the blog posts that accompany your podcast episodes.

Many podcasters find this stage of podcasting a bit of a chore, but there are benefits to spending a bit of time and effort on your show notes. They can help attract new listeners through search traffic, offer a handy summary of what's covered, and provide links and resources to anything mentioned in the episodes.

That said, your podcast needs to be sustainable, or you'll stop doing it. So if you only have the time or energy to do a quick bullet-point summary for each episode, then that's absolutely fine too.

Some podcasters even outsource their show notes to a professional copywriter. So you can still get all the benefits of detailed show notes without writing them yourself, if you have a bit of budget available.

Other podcasters use AI tools like ChatGPT to create first drafts of their show notes. With the right prompts, these won't need a massive amount of editing and can save you a lot of time, not to mention, money.

For a deeper dive into this topic, head on over to thepodcasthost. com/shownotes

Creating an 'About' page

The 'About' page is traditionally the most viewed page of any website, so it's a good idea to take advantage of this. It should never be done as an afterthought.

At first glance, you'd think this would be all about you and your podcast. But the trick here is that it's actually all about your listener. This is where you can pose the questions or problems they're struggling with - and that you're uniquely set up to solve.

On top of listing the benefits they'll get from listening to your podcast, you might also want to create a playlist of your most popular episodes to get them started.

Of course, you will want to add a wee bit about yourself, too. Credibility and personality are important. They're just not the things you'd want to lead with. Again, make it about your listener first, and that's the best way to win them over.

Creating a 'Subscribe' or 'Follow' page

As we've mentioned many times before, your podcast might be consumed in over 100 different places. So sending your listeners to *yourwebsite.com/follow* is better than trying to list them all in your Call to Action.

First and foremost, a 'follow' page could simply say, "Find us wherever you get your podcasts". It doesn't hurt to provide links to some of the bigger platforms, too. Platforms like Apple, Spotify, and Google Podcasts.

If your target audience falls into the "non-techy" bracket, you might also want to go into some detail about what podcasts are, how they work, and how to follow or subscribe to them. Some podcasters even create wee 'how to follow' tutorial videos for the bigger listening platforms, too.

Followers are the lifeblood of your show, so make this as clear and as easy as possible for them, and you're sure to reap the benefits in the long run.

For a deeper dive into this topic, head on over to thepodcasthost. com/sharing

Creating a list of podcast episodes

Some podcasters like to offer a full list of every episode they've published. Others prefer to curate a 'Best Of' list that can help pull in new listeners.

You can do this manually by embedding episode players on a page. Or, your hosting provider might have a feature where you can create this in your podcast player.

You might even choose to create themed pages; for example, here are our listener Q&A episodes, here are our how-to episodes, and here are our quick tip episodes.

Ultimately, you want to turn casual listeners on these pages into followers or subscribers, too. So remember to link to your dedicated 'Follow or Subscribe' page as much as possible here.

Creating a 'Contact' Page

Every podcaster likes listener feedback, but almost every podcaster feels they rarely, if ever, hear from anyone. In many cases, this is simply because they've not made it easy enough.

So instead of reading out your email address, Twitter handle, and Facebook page in your Call to Action, just send them to *yourwebsite.com/contact* to find every way they can connect with you.

You might use a contact form or survey software to better structure and organise your feedback, too.

You could even embed a voice feedback widget from a tool like Telbee or Speakpipe here, and this approach lets you easily collect voice questions and comments that you can use on future episodes.

As a podcaster, it's possible to get regular feedback from your audience - you just need to make sure you're asking for it and making it easy for them.

Sharing buttons

If you're using a WordPress website, then it's worth installing a social media sharing plugin.

There are plenty of good ones, and you can browse them in your 'Add New Plugins' section. When you've installed and activated one of these plugins, you'll see a wee row of social media icons at the bottom of each post and page, and they'll make it easy for anyone to share your episodes to places like Twitter and Facebook with one single click.

It's worth mentioning, too, that if you're using a Podpage website, these buttons will appear on your posts automatically.

Whatever route you go down, though, the main thing is that you're making it easy for your listeners to share your show with others. Over time, this word-of-mouth marketing can have a great impact on your overall podcast growth.

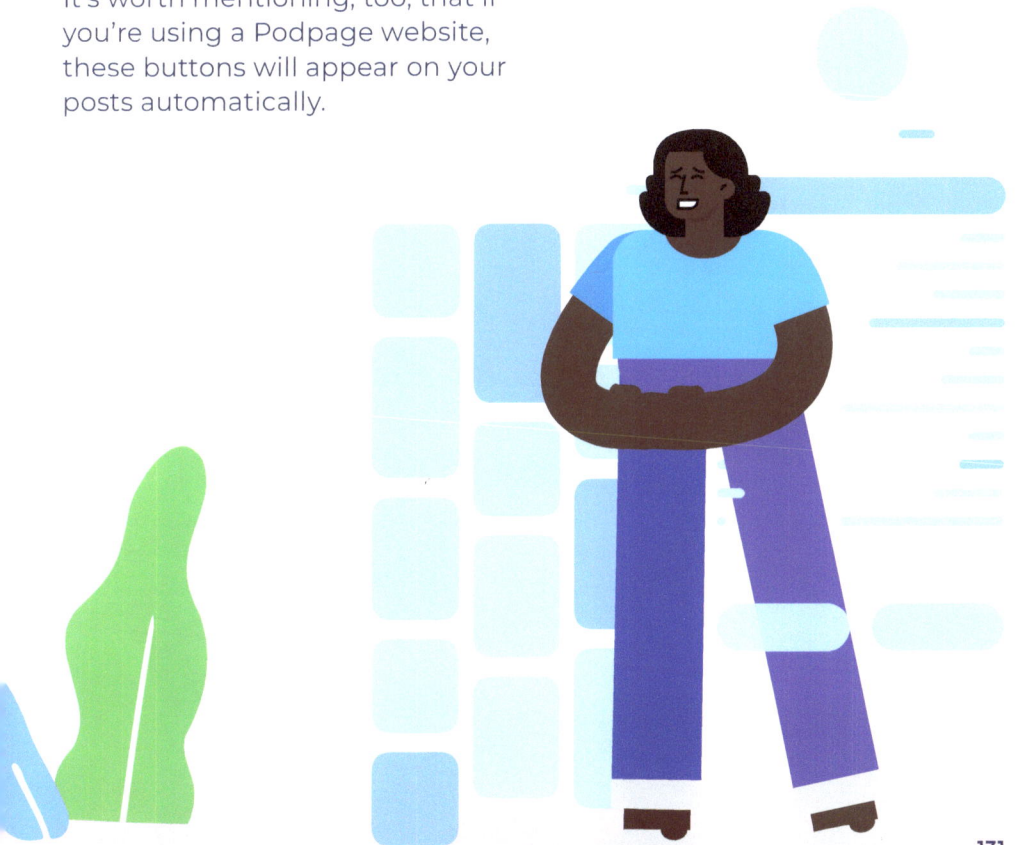

Creating a 'Start Here' page

As podcasters, we can become desensitised to all of the content we've created over a given time.

You might think that your podcast, blog, coaching service, books, and other products all make perfect logical sense. But for someone landing on your site for the very first time, it can be confusing and overwhelming.

Creating a 'Start Here' page is a great way of gently introducing folks to your content. You might combine elements from your 'About' page and full episode list.

Or, you might scrap the other two completely, so there's less confusion. Ultimately, it's all about managing that early journey of potential new listeners. Give them something clear and easy that feels like a quick win for them. Then, show them how to get more.

For a deeper dive into this topic, head on over to thepodcasthost. com/websitetips

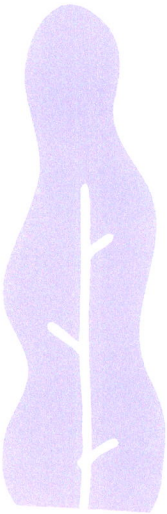

The end? Far from it!

One of the great things about this book is that it's never finished. With your podcast, there will always be aspects of it to tweak, hone, and improve.

Launching a podcast can seem like a daunting process at first, but it's what you do in the following weeks, months, and years that really matters.

Of course, some podcasts do have a natural end, and that's absolutely fine. But there's always another one to start, isn't there? Always another topic, another interest, or another unique angle on something. And, armed with *Finally start your podcast* (and your own ever-growing experience), what better person to tackle them?

Thank you very much for giving this book your time and attention. In a world of infinite and immediately accessible content, we never take it for granted. On the subject of time, hopefully, we've helped save you a lot of it, too.

If *Finally start your podcast* is all you need to launch and grow your show, then we've done our job. But there are other ways for us to help and support you. We'd love to stay in touch.

Our website - **thepodcasthost.com** - is one of the biggest and oldest podcaster resources on the web. We publish new content there every single week, and you can easily keep up with us by subscribing to the Podcraft Pointers newsletter at **thepodcasthost.com/pointers**

We've mentioned our 'Podcast Maker' tool, Alitu, throughout the course of this book, too. With one single subscription and login, you can access call recording, editing, production, music, transcription, hosting, and more, with new features being added all the time. It truly is the ultimate podcasting tool, and we'd love you to test it out for yourself.

Sign up for a seven-day free trial at Alitu.com.

www.ingramcontent.com/pod-product-compliance
Lightning Source LLC
Chambersburg PA
CBHW041711200326
41518CB00005B/191